My Library

TRUE STORIES OF BOOKS, NOOKS, AND FURTIVE LOOKS

Edited by Edward McCann

650 | WHERE WRITERS READ

Founder / Editor • Edward McCann
Executive Producer • Richard Kollath
Senior Editor • Steven Lewis
Marketing and Communications • Jane Kaupp
Design Director • Diane Fokas
Technical Advisor • Conrad Trautmann
Technical Advisor • Stephen Kaupp
Director of Photography • Kevin O'Connor
Videography/Photography • Sara Caldwell
Chief Audio Engineer • Jesse Chason
Copy Editor • Shelley Sadler Kenney

Advisory Committee
Rachel Aydt, Laura Shaine Cunningham,
Angela Davis-Gardner, Joseph Goodrich,
Jeremiah Horrigan, Arif Ilahi Khan, David Masello,
Honor Molloy, Irene O'Garden, John Pielmeier,
Susan Ragusa, James Russek, Angela Derecas Taylor,
Julie Trelstad, and Gretchen Reed

"I have always imagined that Paradise will be a kind of library."

— *Jorge Luis Borges*

ABOUT 650

Libraries everywhere are repositories of information and resources. They help build strong communities by offering free access to meeting space and technology, as well as by offering programs and expertise to people of all backgrounds. But libraries are also the source of many of our memories, and in this volume we've collected a dozen memories from a dozen writers to celebrate National Library Week.

Read650 is a literary nonprofit with a mission to promote writers through live performances that celebrate the spoken word. It's a literary forum featuring two-page, 650-word personal stories that can be performed in five minutes. Our events at theaters, colleges, and libraries around the country are organized around single, broad topics that invite a range of expression, with recorded performances added to a growing digital archive of writers reading their work aloud. The writers and their work will receive additional exposure through podcasts, broadcasts, our YouTube channel, and in printed volumes like the one you hold in your hand—a collection of pieces originally performed on stage at the Ossie Davis Theater in the New Rochelle Public Library.

Read650 features graduate students and grandparents, first-timers and bestsellers. It's all about the writing; it's about the choice of one word over another, about the shape of sentences and paragraphs, the arc of a narrative, the poetry of a unique literary voice. If you love language and enjoy a good story, you've come to the right place. To submit your work or attend our shows, visit our website or Facebook page, and join our mailing list. Please tell your friends about us, and **spread the word about the spoken word.**

Ed McCann

Edward McCann, Founder / Editor

READ650.COM
FACEBOOK.COM/READ650

CONTENTS

My Library

TRUE STORIES OF BOOKS, NOOKS, AND FURTIVE LOOKS

Edited by Edward McCann

LYNN EDELSON

Lynn Edelson is a special educator and family trainer in the New York State Early Intervention Program. She is the mother of two grown sons—a writer and a musician—and says she's fairly certain neither one will ever buy her a beach house. In 2016 she was selected for the New York City cast of the *Listen To Your Mother* show, and for the past five years, she's studied memoir at The Writing Institute at Sarah Lawrence College. Though often accused of writing poetry, Lynn is currently at work on a collection of short stories.

ENCHANTED

Lynn Edelson

When I was in third grade, I took out a book from the school library eleven times in a row. I'd read it, bring it back, and take it out again.

"Are you sure you don't want to try something different today?" Mrs. Inken asked. Mrs. Inken was the elderly librarian who welcomed us into her room each week. She wore her perfect wavy white hair short and was very tall. I loved her.

"Find a seat, children," she'd say quietly as we pulled at the heavy chairs surrounding the long wooden tables. And even the boys, who were bustling with excitement hoping to find books on dinosaurs and space stations, listened to her.

We all did.

"This is a very special place," she told us the first time we entered. "Each of you will be allowed to take six books home, but you have to promise to take very good care of them and return them next week."

We nodded solemnly, waiting for her to give us the signal to get up and grab the books we wanted before anyone else did.

"Again?" she asked me as she went to stamp the manila card

that went into the sleeve in the back of the book.

"Again," I said firmly.

Little Witch was the story of nine-year-old Minx, whose mother was a witch and kept hundreds of jars filled with brightly colored powders on the kitchen shelves. When mixed together, a spell could be cast.

Minx longed to go to school, to have friends, and to be like the other children, but her mother forbade it. She was in charge of making the black spell brew that her mother used to change rude children in the neighborhood into the potted flowers that sat on their windowsill. Every night the witch flew around town on her broomstick, and every day she slept.

Minx watered the flower pots carefully, speaking softly to them. At night when her mother left, she would do her chores—including cooking up toad stew for her mother's morning toast—and then try to find a way to release the enchanted children.

There was also a beautiful mute fairy whom she saw fleetingly in her mirror almost every day, gazing at her lovingly. I don't want to give too much away, but let's just say she looked a lot like Minx.

Something about the powders on the shelves spoke to me. The colors, the potions that could be created, the magic that was within reach. Minx experimented at night, pouring them into a large black kettle. She conjured up pixies and centaurs and nightmares while attempting to undo her mother's evil deeds.

Minx spoke truth to the adults in town who stood in her way. She convinced the principal that she was entitled to be a student, even if she was the witch's daughter. And every morning she risked her mother's wrath as she snuck out the door to go to school, despite not knowing how to read, despite having only one filthy dress to wear that she hand-washed herself.

The kids at school brought her to tears. "Witch's child!" they screamed as they ran away.

Except one—an orphaned girl, who lived with her four brothers and sisters and their great grandmother in a large messy house abounding with joy.

She gave Minx chocolate chip cookies when she was hungry, defended her to others, and admired what a witch's child knew.

She had the courage to be kind and to stand by her friend's side.

I loved visiting with these girls, day after day. They kept me company as I hid in my room, afraid of my father's temper as he slammed doors and spoke to no one.

I ached for their courage, a large black kettle, and the brightly colored powders that could keep me safe—as safe as I felt around Mrs. Inken. As safe as I always felt in the library.

DERIN TANYOL

Derin Tanyol is a curator who lives in the Hudson Valley. She has a Ph.D. in Art History and has published on 19th- and 20th-century art in the *Gazette des Beaux-Arts, Word & Image,* and *19th-Century Art Worldwide,* as well as a monograph on French Surrealist Georges Malkine. She received Fulbright, Kress, and Chateaubriand scholarships for two years of research in Paris, where she discovered pastry products of superior flakiness to their American counterparts—leading to a second career as a pastry chef. Derin is an avid technical rock-climber and has logged over 2000 vertical days on cliffs worldwide. She has taught Art History at Wesleyan University and SUNY New Paltz and is writing a series of personal essays comparing academia and the restaurant industry.

CODES

Derin Tanyol

When I landed in Paris for a two-year art research stint in 1996, stereotypes of the French as elegantly debauched and a little unhealthy were given substance. Billboards publicized Perrier water with a moist, shiny woman, naked but for a Perrier bottle cap seated on each nipple; phone-sex vendors advertised in taxi-stands and subways; smoking was still chic. Once, after I donated blood, the attending physician invited me for a cigarette in the courtyard; he had asked spectacularly vivid questions about my sexual history while a nurse in a form-fitting white pantsuit smiled and took notes.

Everything in France seemed unabashed, loose, free. Everything, that is, except the libraries. While sexually liberated and defiant in the face of lung cancer, the French were tightly wound when it came to call numbers, cataloguing, and the hundreds of words for what, in the US, is simply called a "book." The archives and libraries of Paris house *imprimés* and *manuscrits* and *dossiers* and *folios*, all of which are a *document*—spelled like "document" in English, but if you pronounce the terminal *t*, no one understands. Archival research techniques and all this new vocabulary positioned me as the lost foreigner, acquiring "archive-lingo" in what I hoped to convince people was my mother tongue. It is easy enough to search "Flaubert" in the library catalogue and walk away with *Madame Bovary* under your arm. But finding a postcard Flaubert sent his sister Caroline while writing *Madame Bovary* (its existence suggested via a letter from Caroline to her friend Sophie, cited in a biography by a scholar whose patience with the archive far precedes your own)…this entails blind rummaging through a morass of scrawl-covered scraps, stored in boxes labeled only with long, hyper-punctuated alphanumeric codes. At first, I dreamily caressed the paper inscribed with quill pens whose tips had likely been sucked by my art historical heroes. But romance soon gave way to despair, as actually knowing in which chaotic scrap box to start any given search seemed impossible. I applied often to the librarians who, seated high above the reading room, knew there was a magnificent system of order behind France's Archives Nationales, and that it must be respected.

The acme of order at the Archives Nationales was the Catalogue Room, where insiders and old-timers masterfully unearthed the long codes required to request boxes from storage. The cavernous room was lined with many, many shelves, which supported many more volumes embossed on the spines with numerical series but no words. You open the books to find lists like this:

3746. Painting commissions during the July Monarchy
3747. Ladies' fashions; buggies
3749. The lice epidemic of Calais

It didn't matter that there was no 3748, which would not have cleared things up.

Defeated by these inventories of historical odds and ends, convinced I would never actually write my dissertation, I gave up for a month and explored Parisian debauchery instead of doing my research. Even France's famed sensual pleasures—wine, perfume, lingerie, brothels—are systematized by long-winded, ceremonious regulations that provided deep perspective on the alphanumeric codes. Indeed there *was* a magnificent system of order behind France's Archives Nationales; I just needed a stronger dose of "Frenchness" before I was able to understand it. I even learned to like it. But upon my repatriation at JFK, my American bibliophilic romance was instantly refreshed: Soon, I would be walking down the aisles of the Columbia and CUNY libraries, hand in hand with Library of Congress call numbers and confident in one of the bedrocks of our relationship—the art books, through thick and thin, would always be in the stacks labeled N through NX. This sober, practical, and very un-French approach to classification was native, comforting to me—yet I will return to France over and over, at least until I find Flaubert's postcard.

SANDI SONNENFELD

Sandi Sonnenfeld writes fiction, personal essays, and narrative journalism. With the publication of her memoir, *This Is How I Speak: The Diary of a Young Woman*, Sandi was named a 2002 Celebration Author by the Pacific Northwest Booksellers Association, which recognizes writers whose work merits special notice. Her writing has appeared in more than thirty literary magazines and anthologies, including *Sojourners*, Voices West, *Hayden's Ferry Review*, ACM, Raven Chronicles, Necessary Fiction, *Perigee, Revolution House* and *The Doctor TJ Eckleburg Review*, among others. A graduate of Mount Holyoke College, Sandi holds an MFA in Fiction Writing from the University of Washington, where she won the Loren D. Milliman Writing Scholarship. She currently is working on a historical novel set in seventeenth century Russia. For more, visit https://authorsandisonnenfeld.com.

WILLISTON MEMORIAL LIBRARY, 1985

Sandi Sonnenfeld

During my senior year at Mount Holyoke College, I had a carrel on the north sixth floor stacks of Williston Memorial Library. Six nights a week, I sat in the hardback chair in front of Carrel 622 on the west side of the building, working on my senior thesis—a first attempt at a novel. I was twenty-one years old and desperately longed to be recognized as gifted, hoping that might atone for all my human failings— for being, as my mother often said, "a difficult child."

Sixth North only had five carrels—far fewer than the six other floors that comprised the library tower. I selected this floor less for its isolation and more for its stacks housing the library's American literature collection. I believed somehow that my physical proximity to books by writers like Hawthorne, Melville, Poe, Chopin and Wharton might result in some of their talent rubbing off on me.

When I found myself stuck on a paragraph in my manuscript, laboring for the right line of words, I would stand up from my chair, and stretch my neck and shoulders, pulling my hands over my head. I would use the nearby restroom and sip from the water fountain. Only then would I walk back to the sixth floor stacks and explore the long neatly alphabetized rows of books.

By early October, I had already made it to the Fs. Skipping Faulkner and his three-page-long sentences, my eyes fell on a large red leather-bound volume with *The Short Stories of F. Scott Fitzgerald* embossed in white lettering on the spine.

I had loved *The Great Gatsby* when I read it in high school, but only during one of my creative writing classes had I learned Fitzgerald had published more than one hundred short stories; most appeared in the *Saturday Evening Post*, the proceeds of which paid the bills while he was busy researching and writing his novels.

Now all of Fitzgerald's stories were compiled in one book. Fitzgerald, heralded as a genius at twenty-four, toasted by Paris and New York's intelligentsia at twenty-six, and dead from alcoholism in relative obscurity at forty-four. Fitzgerald, who perhaps wrote the most famous closing line of any American novel, just as Melville wrote the most famous opening one.

I hugged the book to me, carrying it back to my carrel, knowing I would not be working anymore on my manuscript that night. I cracked open the book; a fusty smell and a handful of dust motes arose from the yellowing paper. It had been abandoned a long time. Now it was mine to explore.

As midnight approached, I bookmarked the last Fitzgerald story I had read, placed the volume on the bookshelf that ran across the top of my carrel. I shoved my pen and unfinished manuscript into my backpack to type up what I had written later in the dorm. I switched off the tiny study lamp.

Then, as I did every night, I walked down the two and a half flights to the main reading room. Built in 1905, modeled after London's Westminster Hall in British Parliament, the reading room was long, airy and rectangular, and featured a magnificent hammer-beam ceiling, composed of wooden arches sixty feet high joined together with thick oak beams that served as horizonal supports to hold up the walls. Morris chairs, plush settees with oversized cushions, and long wooden tables with chairs were scattered throughout the cavernous room, offering students a wide range of seating and studying options. Even at night, light streamed through the row of stained-glass windows that ran along the top of the room's south side, each one depicting a different seal of a Seven Sister college, with Mount Holyoke, of course, the eldest sister, in the middle.

As I walked toward the exit, intricately carved angels, wings held high, poised on the end of each oak beam, smiled down on me.

SARAH BRACEY WHITE

Sarah Bracey White is a writer, teacher, and arts consultant. A graduate of Morgan State University and the University of Maryland, she's a former Inaugural Fellow at The Purchase College Writers Center. Published work includes *Primary Lessons: A Memoir*; *The Wanderlust: A South Carolina Folk Tale*, and *Feelings Brought to Surface*, a poetry collection. Her memoir piece, "Freedom Summer," was included in two Simon and Schuster anthologies— *The Children of the Dream* and *Dreaming in Color, Living in Black and White*. Her essays appear in *Aunties: 35 Writers Celebrate Their Other Mother*, *Gardening on a Deeper Level*, and *Heartscapes: True Stories of Remembered Loves*. Other essays have appeared in the *New York Times*, the *Baltimore Afro American* and the *Journal News*. She and her husband live in Ossining, New York.

FOOD FOR THOUGHT

Sarah Bracey White

The only books in the house where I grew up were a big, unabridged dictionary, a 28-volume *World Book Encyclopedia*, and the King James version of the Bible. The paucity would have been understandable if I'd known that my mother grew up in a house without *any* books because her mother was illiterate, and her father could barely read. Mama seldom spoke about her life as a child. Her focus was on teaching school and sending us to school—even when we were sick.

Mama was a school teacher, though she had only two years of college training. Every summer—for fourteen years—she took classes at Morris College, finally earning her diploma two months before my brother, her fifth and last child, was born. To Mama, reading was not for pleasure. Books were a source of knowledge. Knowledge that would change your life. For me, books were an escape from a life I could not change.

Trapped in a small, South Carolina town where the color of my skin barred me from the newly built Carnegie Library on nearby Liberty Street, I reveled in the library on the second floor of Lincoln, the segregated school I attended from grades seven through twelve.

My family's tight budget excluded me from the daily hot lunches sold in Lincoln's cafeteria. Each day after hurriedly eating the bologna sandwich my mother spiced up with hot sauce, I rushed out of the cafeteria and up a short flight of stairs to a place where I could devour as much as I wanted—free of charge. At the top of the stairs, I pushed open the door to a large rectangular room, the mirror image of the cafeteria below—where, instead of tables, rows and rows of evenly spaced, honey-colored, waist-high wooden shelves lined with books of all shapes and sizes marched across the room. Sunlight usually flooded the space through windows that covered three sides of the room. At the windowless end, behind a low counter made of the same blond wood as the shelves, sat a middle-aged woman whose round body and sparkly eyes revealed the satiation that comes from many good meals followed by many good books. I wanted a life just like hers.

On my first visit to the library, I was overwhelmed by the sight of so many books in one place. I wandered from bookshelf to bookshelf, my neck arched at an awkward angle to read the titles without moving the books from their assigned places. The librarian, whom I came to know as Miss Cuthbert, noticed me and called out that it was okay to take books from the shelves. She also said that if I got a library card, I could take up to six home each week. I got a card that very day, and thereafter, proceeded to spend most of lunch hour perusing the collection. I devoured the words in those books as greedily as my classmates gobbled cherry cobbler from their stainless-steel trays.

"At the rate you're going, you'll have read every book in this library before you graduate," Miss Cuthbert once told me.

That was my plan. Lincoln's library fed my love of words and people when I was too poor to buy books. I lost myself in stories about people whose lives were even more hardscrabble than mine—though some were far better. Frequently, the bad lives got better, and those were the lives I longed to inhabit. Those stories seeped into my being, assuring me that I would not always be a poor, colored girl living under separatist rules. They drove me into the arms of learning, propelling me to become a librarian and a writer. Above all, their stories taught me that change was possible.

CINDY CLEMENT CARLSON

Cindy Clement Carlson, has lived in Sandy Hook, Connecticut for eighteen years. She was at work in the Sandy Hook School Library Media Center on the day of the December 2012 shooting. All three of her children attended SHS and her daughter was present on that day.

THE COMMITMENT TO FINDABILITY

Cindy Clement Carlson

I am reading *The Library Book* by Susan Orlean. She describes a library's need for order and proper shelving, observing that "the commitment to findability is absolute." A misshelved book may as well be thrown into the trash. School librarians ask their students not to reshelve books they've browsed to avoid dolphin nonfiction in mythology, or panda books in the origami section.

After you've listened to gunshots kill twenty kids and six teachers, the library can help you get yourself back in order, too.

After the December 2012 shooting at Sandy Hook School, every book and magazine in the library media center was packed by professional library movers, trucked to a nearby mothballed school, and unpacked. Every Kindle, bookmark, and morning meeting rug was taken from the sacred chaos of that building and brought to a former middle school in Monroe.

Over a wretched, extended winter break marked by funerals, our staff of three estimated how high an elementary student could reach on a middle school shelf. We evaluated our storage closet for its capacity to shelter students from gunfire. We unpacked familiar posters and signs all while learning how to lock the doors quickly.

Then, first day in Monroe for the students. *Every aspect of school has changed yet the library can remind you who you are.* Remember how much you liked the stuffed dragon? It's still on top of the non-fiction shelf! Remember the bin of princess books? Yes, here it is! Sharks? Right here in Dewey 597.3!

Library cards, also brought to Monroe from Sandy Hook, were out on our new circulation desk, by the computer as always. You're a third grader, your card is still blue. There's the corner where the lamination has been picked each year since the card was earned as a kindergartener. And yes, hearing that metal water bottle clatter to the floor in the hall was terrifying; let's wheel the library cart around so we'll know what that sounds like.

Most satisfying was fulfilling a hold placed in the old school. With effortful handwriting, students had filled out hold slips in Sandy Hook to request books already checked out. When those books were returned to the new school, I silently thanked the upset parents who had the presence of mind to remember it was library day and enthusiastically informed students that their request was in!

Never mind that the staff was accounting for books left in classrooms where the shooting had occurred, that we wrapped a rubber band around a stack of twenty library cards of students who had died, that we threw away overdue notices for students who had lost a sibling. For our young patrons we focused on what was consistent and still in place. Last night your mother explained how girls from your Brownie troop had died, but the next morning in the library here are the RookieRead-Abouts in the cart as always, square edges, lined up in Dewey order. Your bus stop has two fewer kids each morning but in the library the tent card that shows your place at the table is propped up to greet you in January just like it did in December.

That first winter, Martin Luther King Day and President's Day came quickly. Tucked in the back room for now were the books that described those who died by shooting. But look! The Valentine books we've been displaying for years! Come check out *Clifford's First Valentine's Day* and Fancy Nancy: Heart to Heart just like you did when you were a second grader.

We strove to maintain our traditions. Caldecott Award Day! Nutmeg Novel Reveal Day! Six Caldecott Days later, we're still putting the pieces of ourselves back together as a town and a school community. I hope the library helped some of these kids find who they were before the shooting. The commitment to findability is absolute.

DWIGHT E. WATSON

Dwight Watson's writing appears in journals including *The Chronicle Review, Ars Medica : A Journal of Medicine, the Arts and Humanities., Still Point Arts Quarterly,* The Dead Mule Society of Southern Literature, Review Americana, Poydras Review, and Cha: An Asian Literary Journal. The author of *The Blacksmith's Book, Eden Creek: A Play in Five Monologues,* and *Dapple Gray,* his plays and monologues appear in several books and monologue collections. The recipient of the McClain-McTurnan- Arnold Excellence in Teaching Award, he is Professor of Theater Emeritus and Lafollette Distinguished Professor of the Humanities at Wabash College.

IT'S STORY TIME

Dwight E. Watson

My granddaughter and I enter the library. We walk through the scanner, past the circulation desk, and beyond the computer lab occupied by city residents searching the web. We are on our way to Story Time for toddlers.

Today's library isn't the library of my youth. Then, it was a quiet place with only the sound of rolling carts and the scrape of book covers as the librarians returned books to their proper shelves. Now, the library is a command center of activities from ESL classes to Internet 101.

My granddaughter tugs my hand. Story Time is on the third floor.

We begin the climb to the children's library. I'm thinking of gravity. Steps are designed for adults, not short-legged children. Her lift to climb is twice mine, and yet, unfazed by gravity, she powers upward. We reach the third floor.

Story Time is crowded with toddlers and grandparents. The storyteller is preparing audio and visual aids. A pleasant woman, she's a seasoned librarian. On another day, I imagine her wearing a grey wool suit and black Oxford shoes, her hair coiled in a bun (but, maybe I am thinking of the librarian of my youth). This librarian is of normal height, weighs more than some, with a smile that doesn't break. Today, she's dressed comfortably in a pair of drawstring pants, an outfit perfect for the physicality of Story Time.

Somewhat short-of-breath, she executes her lesson plan carefully. To be fair, her Story Time is engaging. She takes care in explaining the topic to the children— "The Human Body." "Look at all the working parts," she wiggles her fingers. She quizzes them on the function of the eyes, ears, and more, and moves them through a series of activities—Flash Cards, Simon Says!, and Body Balancing.

We are told to "Stand up, Sit Down!" Then, the librarian ends Story Time with a familiar song: "Head, Shoulders, Knees, and Toes."

With each mention of anatomy, she points to the body part. One little boy wanders—stepping away from his caregiver. He circles the librarian, and, in slow motion, lifts and lowers his "wings," and fades away from the mothership to which he is no longer tethered. The librarian is undisturbed by the boy's independence. My granddaughter seems more attracted to the boy's journey than to the calisthenics offered by the librarian, who, presses on…

"Head, shoulders, knees, and toes."

Insisting that the children (and caregivers by default) join her in song and gesticulation, all, excluding the one space walker, do.

"Head, shoulders, knees, and toes. Knees and toes."

Unlike my grandchild who moves easily through the appointment of each body part, I do not bend well in the middle and my "knees and toes" get only a passing acknowledgement as if I am saying to them, "I see you there."

"Head, shoulders, knees and toes." "Knees and toeooos." Confidently, I have no problem pointing to the parts that follow:

"And eyes and ears and mouth and nose."

In fact, we all, except the space walker, are feeling good about the song as the chorus of kids and grandparents join in, joyously, following our grand librarian, full voiced, to the song's crescendo:

"Head, shoulders, knees and toes."

The librarian bends to express the last repeat of "knees and toes," and as she lifts the song to its conclusion, she stands straight up, while her pants fall to her knees. To her kneeeees.

There is nothing but whiteness. Blinded by bloomers, I avert my eyes, as do others, except for the innocent children, who carry on. The librarian, reaches down, retrieves her pants, and, with a quick tie of the drawstring, finishes the class, with, "See you next week." We applaud, file out of Story Time, leaving our librarian to pick up the pieces.

Descending the steps from the third floor presents less of a challenge. Now, we are friends with gravity; friends of the library.

ANDI ROSENTHAL

Andi Rosenthal is the author of the novel *The Bookseller's Sonnets*, which was a Hadassah Brandeis Institute book club selection and a National Jewish Book Council "Book of Note." Andi has published personal essays in Kveller, ScaryMommy, and *Reform Judaism* magazine. From 2003 to 2008, Andi was the writer of a first-person column featured on InterfaithFamily.com and in the *Westchester Jewish Chronicle*. She most recently published a selection of poetry in Volume nine of *The Westchester Review*. In her professional life, Andi serves as a community mobilizer for UJA-Federation of New York and is also an accomplished musician. A lifelong resident of Westchester County, she lives in New Rochelle.

A PAGE OUT OF TIME/LIFE

Andi Rosenthal

While most of my friends preferred Carvel or old Eli's candy store at the corner of Mill Road and Parsons Place, my hangout was the Eastchester Library. Built in 1967, at the height of the space race, it had a futuristic look to it, a sleek white monument to the incurably curious.

Our town's very first instance of mid-century modern architecture crowned the hill on Oakridge Place, its bright lines a sharp contrast to the sun-mellowed, friendly red-brick apartment houses next door. Inside, a glassed-in stairway led to the main floor, its ceilings dotted with dancing Calder-style mobiles. The reading rooms, with their book-lined aisles and twin silvery staircases to the top floor stacks, seemed to beckon to the heavens.

My library was a refuge, a respite from the vagaries of childhood fads and fashions. It was safe; certainly no self-respecting school bully would be caught dead there. More importantly, it was filled with books: those gifts of words destined to ignite the imagination of an aspiring author or soothe the hurt feelings of a seventh-grade outcast. Almost from the moment that I received my first library card,

I craved the tranquility of a life surrounded by stories.

In 1985, my fifteenth summer, I was hired as a page; my haven now became my workplace. For a geeky, bespectacled teenager fascinated with history, the eighties were intolerable: an era of bad cologne, three-minute music videos, and too many cable channels. History was starting to feel vaguely disposable. In general, 1985 was an environment hostile to the bookish. I needed an escape.

That was when I discovered a secret portal to the past.

In the library's basement, next to the service elevator, was a door no one ever opened. Intrigued, one morning, I abandoned my cart of returned books and quietly entered. I breathed in the smell of dust and old ink. As my eyesight adjusted to the low light, I saw boxes and boxes of files on the steel shelves. Reaching inside, I pulled out a magazine called *Look*. Its cover seemed to call out to me from the sixties—a girl in an orange minidress, white boots, elaborately curled hair, pale lipstick, and a tracing of flower petals surrounding her wide, dark eyes.

I discovered defunct magazines I had never heard of, titles long out of print. Of course, there were familiar issues like *Vogue* and *Seventeen* and *Cosmopolitan*. But I had no interest in those old dusty, fluffy stories about prom dresses and boyfriends. Instead, I read about war and culture, music and politics—a cascade of turbulent decades unfurling in real time.

As the summer days passed, I would find time each day to slip down to the basement. I read not only about the Kennedy assassinations and the Beatles' arrival in America, but I also read the less monumental stories that were published on my parents' birthdays, the week of their wedding, the day I was born. I wanted to read the headlines that had once perhaps captured their attention from a distant newsstand. Even though I knew how so many of these stories ended, I wanted to read them, in their time, with their eyes.

Reading *Life* and *Look* and *Harper's Bazaar* and *Time* gave me access to history while in its present day, captured in those thin fragile pages. They allowed me to hold the past in my hands, helped me to understand the days of those I loved when they were my age, young and wondering, and discovering their lives.

The magazine room no longer exists. A year ago, I stood in that space, now an auditorium, giving a book talk as a writer of historical fiction whose work is rooted in uncovering the details of the past. But once upon a time, I found out what it felt like to touch the past before it was scanned, saved to the cloud, digitized, and discarded. Intangible.

JEFFREY PODOLSKY

A graduate of Brown University, **Jeffrey Podolsky** has worked as a reporter and editor at *People* magazine, *George* magazine, *Tatler* magazine in London as well as the *Sunday Times Magazine* of London. He was a founding editor of *WSJ.* magazine, has written about men's style at *Barron's*, and appeared as a commentator on WSJ.com A frequent contributor to *W* magazine, *Vanity Fair*, and T: the New York Times Style Magazine, Jeffrey enjoys nothing more than reading aloud to his two incorrigible mutts, Alibi and her pup, Junior.

STUDYING MY FATHER

Jeffrey Podolsky

My father's library furnished me with a zest for the written word, culminating in a close connection to libraries and to him. He was a foreboding figure. Never more so than while sequestered in his library in my childhood home in Detroit. No one dared knock on its stained-glass door. We could feel his presence, but not much else. He could sense the slightest step. Not that I ever heard him raise his voice. His mere presence unravelled you.

For reasons I've yet to fully understand, my father granted me access to his sanctum, a place I would come to learn—to which he needed to go for a clarity that was absent in his life with my mother— who was often lost in an inebriated fog of illness. I spent endless nights with a toy car on an Aubusson rug. He left me alone with my imagination. I was a captive audience: a five-year-old enveloped in a body cast, the result of a freak fall.

It was a lucky break, in some ironic way. I loved staying up past midnight with my insomniac father. The comfort of wood-paneled walls displaying the Oxford English Dictionary, the Grove Music Dictionary, both the Old and New Testaments and *his* bible on wine by

Frank Schoonmaker. Epic poetry by Chaucer and Homer sat opposite the latest paperbacks by Irwin Shaw, Philip Roth, and John Updike.

Come midnight, he abandoned his dictaphone and partners desk for a leather wingchair and a book, scrawling questions and comments on each page. He sniffed and sipped a rounded belly-glass of XO Armagnac while reading to the sonorous and heart-rending rhythms of T. S. Eliot or Billie Holiday. I lay blanketed below in a steady rotation of Churchillian cigars and various shaped pipes.

By the time I was thirteen, I'd become an outcast. The odd kid out at a boarding school where I spent most of my first term hanging by my boxers on a nail. I found refuge from "the great wedgie" at the Choate library. A Georgian building built by Andrew Mellon, its blue-blooded warmth of fireplaces, chintz-covered chairs and works by students such as John Dos Passos, Edward Albee, Adlai Stevenson, and John F. Kennedy felt like something my father might take to and eased a wrenching homesickness.

At college, a different alienation set in. An isolation personified by the cold exterior of the Brown University library, aptly-named "The Rock". Each night, its interior became the campus social hub, where students were acutely aware of their hallowed status and carried themselves accordingly with a cool self-possession. Inside and out, the library—the one place I could always find solace—now terrified me.

It took another library, though, for me to realize my professional calling. While flipping through *Time* magazine in Boston's neoclassical Athenaeum soon after I'd graduated, I realized my desire to become a newspaper reporter, an epiphany so emphatic that I heard a stereophonic "Shhh!" in the space upon pronouncing my desire to be the next editor of *Time*.

I settled for a less lofty role at *People*, where I became resident expert on royal bulimia. But while at The Time-Life Building, I underwent a life-defining circumstance: a trip to the "morgue," that mythi-cal-yet-real repository of clips about everyone from Fatty Warbucks to Edward Teller. Information on a scale I'd never before seen.

So entranced have I remained by my father's reading habits and his embrace of words and their meaning, that when I look out the window at my neighborhood library—the Jefferson Market branch in the West Village—and hear the tonal chimes from its medievalesque clocktower, I see my father glancing down at his pocket watch. The library nook I've created in my apartment can't rival that of my father's, but I do imagine him taking his place in one of the chairs I have and our talking together, two adults, about the words surrounding us.

BARBARA JOSSELSOHN

Barbara Josselsohn is a freelance writer and novelist. Her articles and essays appear in the *New York Times, Parents* magazine, *American Baby* magazine, *Writer's Digest,* and *Westchester* magazine. Online you can see her work at WorkingMother.com, GrownandFlown. com, NextAvenue.org, Cheapism.com, and TheManifestStation.net. Last October, she appeared alongside eight other writers in "Every Family's Got One," a staged reading at the Cinema Arts Centre in Huntington, New York. Her novel is *The Last Dreamer.* Barbara teaches novel writing at the Sarah Lawrence College Writing Institute and other venues. Visit her online at www.BarbaraSolomonJosselsohn. com and Facebook.com/BarbaraSolomonJosselsohnAuthor. You can also follow her @BarbaraJoss on twitter.

NANCY DREW AND THE MYSTERY OF THE MISSING BOOKS

Barbara Josselsohn

It was a decision worthy of Solomon, but it landed on my twelve-year-old lap: Should I fail English? Or throw Mrs. Flucager under the bus?

Mrs. Flucager was the children's librarian at Syosset Public Library and the most magical adult I'd ever encountered. She wore white blouses with Peter Pan collars and flouncy skirts and had straight black hair that hugged her head like a bowl. She looked like she never completely grew up. I figured a life among kids' books could have that effect.

But the most wondrous thing about Mrs. Flucager was her penchant for recommendations. She knew exactly what each kid would want. The books she selected for me always revolved around a quiet, well-behaved schoolgirl who asserted her independence to rescue someone in need. It was the kind of heroine I yearned to be.

That spring, my English class studied journalism. Our teacher, Mr. Feinstein, thought investigative reporters were the noblest of people, and he urged us to pursue truth at any cost. Our final project was to interview someone we admired. Of course, I chose Mrs. Flucager.

Also, around this time, my mother began working as a library assistant. One evening, I overheard her tell my dad about a tiff at work. A patron had asked Mrs. Flucager for the Nancy Drew section, and Mrs. Flucager said there wasn't any. "Those books are *junk*," she told the woman. "I don't carry junk."

My mom sounded amused by the incident, but it stopped me cold. I'd read some Nancy Drews we owned at home, and they were very nice books. Nancy was smart and determined, as in *The Hidden Staircase*, where she stumbled through a trapdoor, landed in the pitch-black cellar, squeezed through a narrow passageway and, armed only with a flashlight, discovered the secret staircase that revealed the burglar who'd terrorized the two elderly widows. Why was that junk? And more important, why was Mrs. Flucager banning books, anyway? Mr. Feinstein would tell me to call her out...

But, no! I thought. Mrs. Flucager was someone I loved. Could I actually accuse her of censorship and make her look bad? On the other hand, could I brush this off? Would Woodward and Bernstein let her off the hook? What was I going to do?

Still unsure, I arrived at her office on interview day and started down my questions: Where did she grow up? Brooklyn, she answered. Why did she become a children's librarian? She was passionate about reading. How did she choose which books to carry, and were there any she wouldn't? I held my breath, hoping I'd misunderstood my mom.

No such luck. "I don't carry junk," she said. "Like Nancy Drew. That's *junk*."

A slew of follow-up questions aligned in my mind like well-trained soldiers: What made those books junk? What criteria did she use? What if kids wanted them anyway? Was censorship *ever* okay?

I opened my mouth...and tried...but it wasn't happening. I

didn't have the stomach to put Mrs. Flucager on the spot. I simply wrote "No junk" in my notebook. Then I asked another question.

Two days later I submitted my paper, and when Mr. Feinstein returned it, he jabbed his finger at that word, *junk.* "Why didn't you press her?" he said. "You missed the whole story!"

I nodded and looked for the red "F." He had been kind: "B-". Still, it was the lowest grade I ever received.

I never showed Mrs. Flucager my paper. I didn't want to explain that grade. But even so, I regarded it as a badge of honor. Like Nancy, I had descended into the darkness and emerged intact, if slightly bruised. I'd sacrificed my grade and withstood a teacher's disapproval to protect the reputation of my beloved librarian.

Finally, I'd acted like the heroine in a novel – a so-called "junky" one, but a novel nevertheless.

I had Mrs. Flucager to thank for that.

DAVID MASELLO

David Masello moved to New York more than thirty years ago from Evanston, Illinois, and he has made his living as a writer and editor ever since. He began his career as a nonfiction book editor at Simon & Schuster and held senior editorial positions at many magazines, including *Travel & Leisure*, *Art & Antiques*, and *Town & Country* (where he was features editor). He's currently executive editor of *Milieu*, a magazine about design and architecture. He's a widely published essayist and poet, with pieces appearing in the *New York Times*, *Salon*, *Best American Essays*, and numerous literary and art magazines. His plays have been produced and performed by the Manhattan Repertory Theatre, Jewish Women's Theatre, Big Apple Theatre Festival, and Fresh Fruit Festival. He is the author of two books about art and architecture.

SCALE AND EFFECT

David Masello

Just a morning later and I couldn't remember if the house was hexagonal or octagonal. The frame dwelling occupies a crossroads, so quiet there's no stop sign, and it drew us across the campus like a lodestone, as if the glinting minerals in the schist of its border walls possessed magnetic charge.

My friend and I felt a sudden love for its shape and scale. "I could live there," I said to Jonathan, as did he, but with a different tone. We circled the property, petted its warped planks, tried the door—locked—and inhaled the scent of clipped hedges ringing it like a trimmed beard.

We'd seen the house after he and I disassembled a modest exhibition he'd mounted in the college library. My friend is an expert in monumental sculpture, forms mostly abstract, positioned on office building plazas, anchored in fields in sculpture parks. Some loom heroically, others register as mere shadows.

Because he's a book designer by profession whose favored shapes are serifs and arials, Jonathan had arrayed in glass display cases in the undergraduate library vintage pamphlets and brochures, photos and sketches, letters relating to the making of monumental steel sculpture. The publications dated from the 1960s, when most of the works were fabricated and assumed their roles as public art. My friend wanted me to see his show and he needed someone to help him disassemble it, carry the materials back to New York by train from the upstate campus.

After I'd examined with exaggerated enthusiasm the printed matter backdropped by maroon velvet—not a single student joining us to look—Jonathan unlocked the cases and we began the gathering. He'd asked me to spend the Saturday with him, someone whose presence had become as big to me as a sculpture, but to whom I couldn't confess such, without a monumental effect.

That's one of the great things about falling in love, requited or unrequited: You learn to love what the other person does. Suddenly, I notice monumental sculpture I encounter—a Calder stabile whose red, yellow, and blue fins stab a lawn; a glossy-yellow beam drawn across a green meadow in an upstate sculpture park; the black cube at Astor Place to which I give a push and watch it rotate.

As Jonathan and I gathered the ephemera, brittle with age, documenting works that endure, I realized scale has no relation to effect. Here was an exhibition in a library about monumental things recounted in diminutive ways. Here was a man unaware of the scale of my feelings. I'd read that each cell within us has six feet of DNA, strands, if laid end-to-end, would reach 67 billion miles. Each of us has something in us that reaches that far.

I held the hinged glass cases as Jonathan scooped up materials, the panes capturing our smiling faces, ghostly reflections and refractions. If I could sculpt, cast a monumental work on the scale of those recounted in the publications, this collaboration between us is what I'd render. Absent such talents, that scene remains preserved inside of me, on permanent exhibit only to myself.

Jonathan was sad his show was over, aware too, that its effect on the students hadn't exactly been monumental. So, when we exited the library, we found ourselves drawn to that historic house, lingering. We instructed the cab to come there to take us to the station. We each looked at the house with different longings. I imagined the unfamiliar and, likely, lovely dimensions within that I wished I could occupy with him.

My friend had become monumental to me, so much so that it overwhelmed our friendship.

But that day, in the backseat of the cab, I suggested he come to my place for dinner and that during the train ride back we could finish the Sunday crossword puzzle, solve it together, sitting side-by-side filling in the grid, and then return to where I live.

KRYSTIA BASIL

Krystia Basil has been a producer in the film & TV industry since 2005. In 2015 she co-founded the company Poplewaca Productions through which she develops scripts and show concepts. She was inspired to write for children after having two of her own. Her first children's picture book will be released in the fall of this year. Originally from Chennai, India, she has been trying to figure out being a "New Yorker' for the last fifteen years.

MY LIBRARY

Krystia Basil

If I could I would choose to live in a cocoon of books stacked ten high and twenty deep. If I could I would choose to die amongst books—words swirling around my soul skeptical of another heaven. All my life, libraries in all forms have been my true church, reading my true religion.

This love of reading is my mother's living legacy to me. Newly married and settling down in the sprawling metropolis of Madras, the first thing her husband discovered was that he had committed to a library visit once a week. These were libraries wherein you paid a small fee per book, per day. This expense would find a permanent place in the monthly budget. But riding his scooter to the library, with his young wife primly sitting pillion, impeccably dressed in a chiffon sari, her one hand holding onto the spare wheel mounted to the rear, the other hand wrapped across his hammering, happy heart, the effort and the expense had been worth it.

Three kids later, the tradition continued. On day one of summer my father knew to prepare for the hour-long journey to the biggest and best lending library in the city, *Eswari*. We now had a family van, our trusted Maruti Suzuki. We carried with us two large jute bags with sturdy wooden handles. They would come back filled to the brim with novels for my mother—Danielle Steele and Mary Higgins Clark jostling with Stephen King and John Grisham. For us kids it was Archie and the gang, spunky Nancy Drew and those groovy Hardy Boys.

But it wasn't just the lending libraries of Madras that fed my reading frenzy. When we visited the cosmopolitan city of Bangalore, my cousins introduced me to another super sleuth, Trixie Belden. Klutzy and awkward but smart and fearless, Trixie solved mysteries around her hometown Sleepyside-on-the-Hudson. I related to her growing up, I still want to *be* her when I'm all grown up. And the series is absolutely why I live near the Hudson River.

In the seaside town of Pondicherry, my other cousins maintained a small library in their home, stacked with back issues of *Reader's Digest* as well as books on the adventures of adolescent girls in boarding schools like Saint Clare's, Malory Towers, and the alpine Chalet School. Oh, how I longed to be a boarder sharing tuck boxes during covert midnight feasts.

When I came to the United States for my Master's degree, my first winter in the bucolic university town of Oxford, Ohio, knocked me near dead. As undergrads stocked up for snowstorms with giant bags of pretzels and six-packs of beer, I shored up my spirit by heading to the cavernous school library and checking out armloads of books on every subject that had ever caught my imagination growing up. In my cozy off-campus room I set up a third-hand bookshelf that I lovingly lined with my library books. I racked up substantial fines I had to pay before I could graduate, a small price for two years of literal literary immersion.

To date, my most delightful discovery about the US of A is not the jalapeno poppers from Arby's or the lemon-glazed doughnuts from Krispy Kreme. It is the very fact that public libraries exist. To be part of a community that prioritizes access to books the same as access to water—I do not take this for granted, especially now.

My parents taught me well, and I'm doing the same for their grandchildren. It is now my treasured tradition to head to my local library with my kids in tow. After story time, I read in a rocking chair while my kids lose themselves in the children's nook. We leave with far too many books to carry.

EDWARD MCCANN

Edward McCann is an award-winning writer/producer and the founder and editor of Read650, a literary forum that celebrates the spoken word with live events in New York City and elsewhere. A frequent contributor to *Milieu* magazine, Ed's features and essays have been published in many literary journals, anthologies, and national magazines, including the *Sun, Country Living*, the *Irish Echo, Better Homes & Gardens, Good Housekeeping* and others. His essay, "Pregnant Again," was selected for the anthology, *Listen To Your Mother*, published by Putnam. He lives and writes in the Hudson River Valley.

THE BOOKMOBILE

Edward McCann

I grew up the youngest of a large family in a small town that just happens to be located in a big city. During the early seventies, my southern Queens hometown of Broad Channel—the only inhabited island in Jamaica Bay—was a provincial backwater sharing more in common with a fishing village in Newfoundland than with anything in New York City. During my childhood, kids made their own fun on boardwalks and unpaved roads, playing ringalevio or smacking a handball off the side wall of the Hildebrand's funeral parlor on East Fourteenth Road. Our soundtrack was the cry of seagulls and the roar of jets taking off from nearby JFK International Airport. With its distant skyline visible to the west across the bay, Manhattan was as remote to me as the city of Oz. And while Broad Channel had plenty of otherworldly charm in its sandbars and horseshoe crabs, attracting nature lovers and hardcore birdwatchers to its wildlife sanctuary, during my childhood the town had no movie theater, no public park, no youth center, and no library.

We had things to read at home, of course—*The Jungle Book*, *Swiss Family Robinson*, the *Reader's Digest*, but not much to hold the interest of a little kid for very long.

I was six years old in 1970, a first grader in Mrs. Wortman's class at PS 47. With help from Mom and my sister, Mary, I'd learned early to read and to write, so I was already bored and disruptive while some of my classmates were still learning to "sound out" words on the page. I needed more to do, more to read.

One day, something magical happened that altered the course of my childhood: Mrs. Wortman took our class on a local, walking field trip, traveling the short distance to Cross Bay Boulevard, where a sleek, gleaming bookmobile sat parked in front of O'Sullivan's Pharmacy.

Excited and anxious, I climbed the fold-out steps at the vehicle's rear, passing through a portal into another realm: a remarkable carpeted and air-conditioned library on wheels. I scanned the walls of shelves lining the interior, inhaling the scent of all those books. An expansive, wrapround windshield allowed daylight to flood the cabin of this amazing, tricked-out rolling library—a kind of miracle that seemed to have come to town from the future.

Its driver was also the librarian, and she swivelled her seat to face us at the narrow checkout desk. There, she issued me my very first, very own library card that I used to check out an armload of bright yellow Curious George titles.

What a thrill it was to carry those books back to school and then be allowed to take them home—my library books from my library! I read and re-read them and traded them the next time for more books from a seemingly limitless, bottomless source—one of the most indelible joys of my young life.

Having my very first, very own library card meant it was also time for my very first, very own wallet, a light-colored billfold with lacing around its edges that featured an embossed cowboy on a rearing horse. I felt very grown up each time I reached for my wallet to present my VIP library card at the bookmobile checkout.

There were dozens of branches of the Queens Public Library, but until age twelve and sixth grade, I never went to any of them; I went instead, in all seasons and in all weather conditions, to the bookmobile. As years passed, I moved on from Curious George and Dr. Seuss to *Charlotte's Web* and the Hardy Boys, entering stories and dimensions that expanded my imagination and my appetite for more.

The immediate surroundings of my island hometown may have had their limits, but the entire world opened up to me in the bookmobile, my once-a-week miracle library on wheels.

ACKNOWLEDGMENTS

In addition to the contributors to this volume, we thank the Friends of the New Rochelle Public Library, which raises dollars through extraordinary hands-on efforts in "recycling" books and other materials—money that funds nearly five hundred public programs conducted at the main library each year. **Nrpl.org/friends-of-the-nrpl**

Our gratitude to the volunteers of The New Rochelle Public Library Foundation for raising resources and providing advocacy to keep the library vibrant, up-to-date, and able to serve the diverse needs of the New Rochelle community. **Nrplfoundation.org**

We appreciate the New Rochelle Council on the Arts (NRCA) for its generous support of Read650, and for stimulating and encouraging the study and presentation of the performing and fine arts. Throughout the year, NRCA sponsors many exhibitions, theatrical productions, dance recitals, film screenings, lectures, and concert series. **NewRochelleArts.org**

Special thanks to nonprofits consultant and strategist Susan Ragusa, whose free monthly Nonprofits TALK strengthens the nonprofit community in New York's Hudson River Valley through workshop/trainings that address common organizational challenges. **SusanJRagusa.com**

READ650.COM

INFO @READ650.COM
FACEBOOK.COM/READ650

BLOOD

STORM

RETRIBUTION

THE OMEGA DETECTIVE: BOOK 1

KEN GARDNER